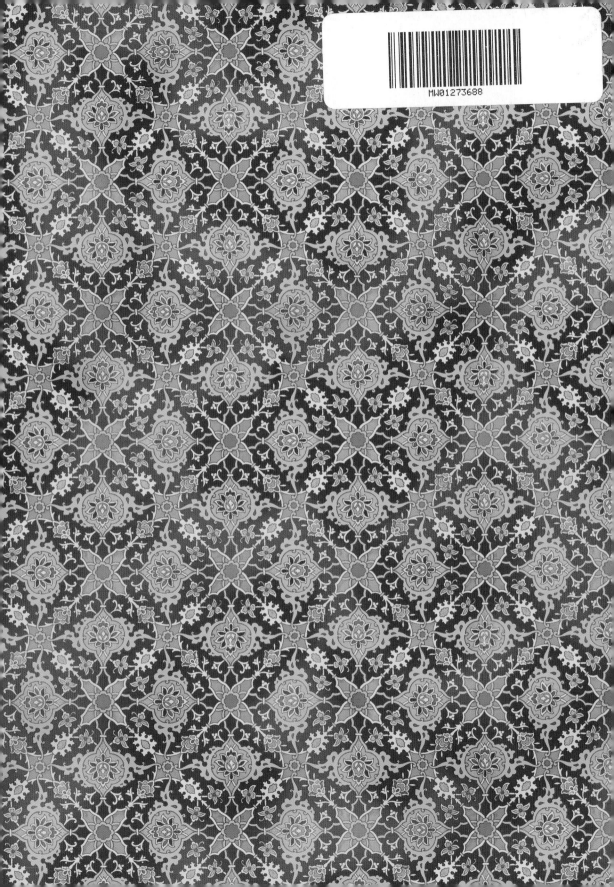

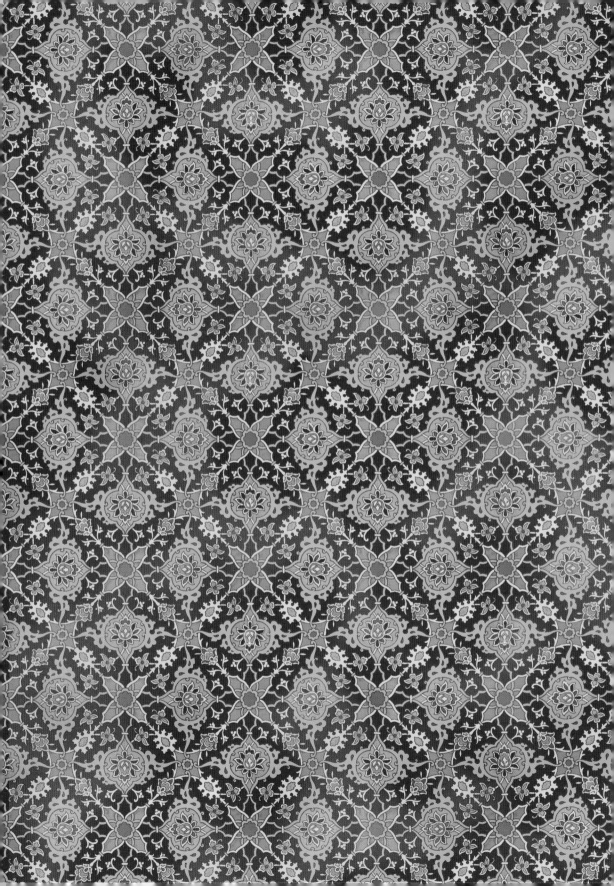

You can't come into the room without my feeling all over me a ripple of flame, and if, wherever you touch me, a heart beats under your touch, and if, when you hold me, nd I don't speak, it's because all the words in me seem to have become throbbing pulses.
—*Edith Wharton*

_____

_____

_____

_____

_____

_____

_____

_____

_____

_____

_____

_____

_____

_____

_____

_____

_____

_____

_____

_____

_____

_____

_____

_____

Doubt that the stars are fire
Doubt that the sun doth move
Doubt truth to be a liar
But never doubt I love.
—*William Shakespeare*

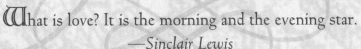

What is love? It is the morning and the evening star.
—*Sinclair Lewis*

_____

_____

_____

_____

_____

_____

_____

_____

_____

_____

_____

_____

_____

_____

_____

_____

_____

_____

_____

_____

_____

_____

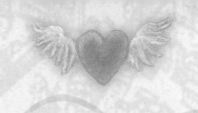

Pains of love be sweeter far
Than all the other pleasures are.
—*John Dryden*

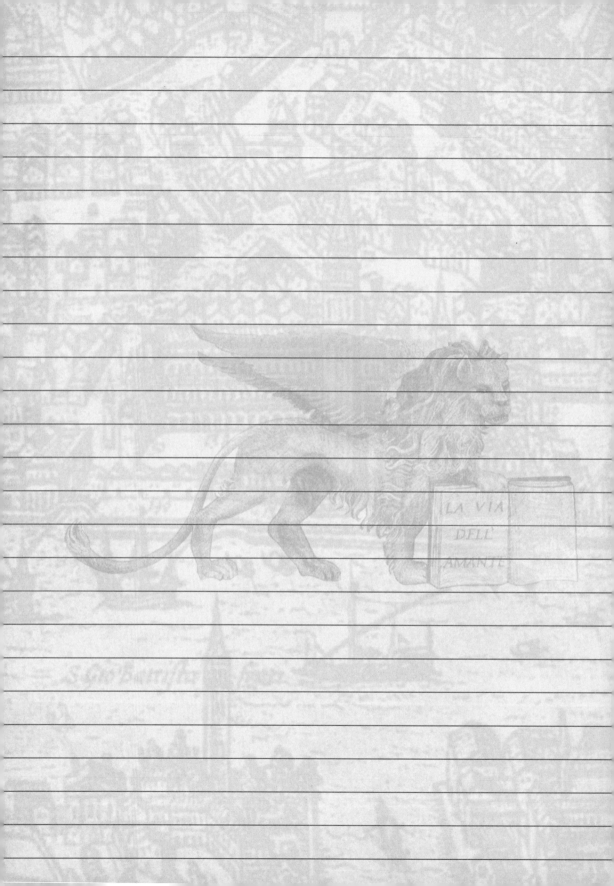

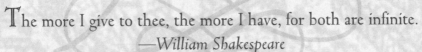

The more I give to thee, the more I have, for both are infinite.
—*William Shakespeare*

_____

_____

_____

_____

_____

_____

_____

_____

_____

_____

_____

_____

_____

_____

_____

_____

_____

_____

_____

_____

_____

_____

_____

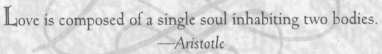

Love is composed of a single soul inhabiting two bodies.
—*Aristotle*

The best and most beautiful things in the world cannot be seen or even touched—
they must be felt with the heart.
—*Helen Keller*

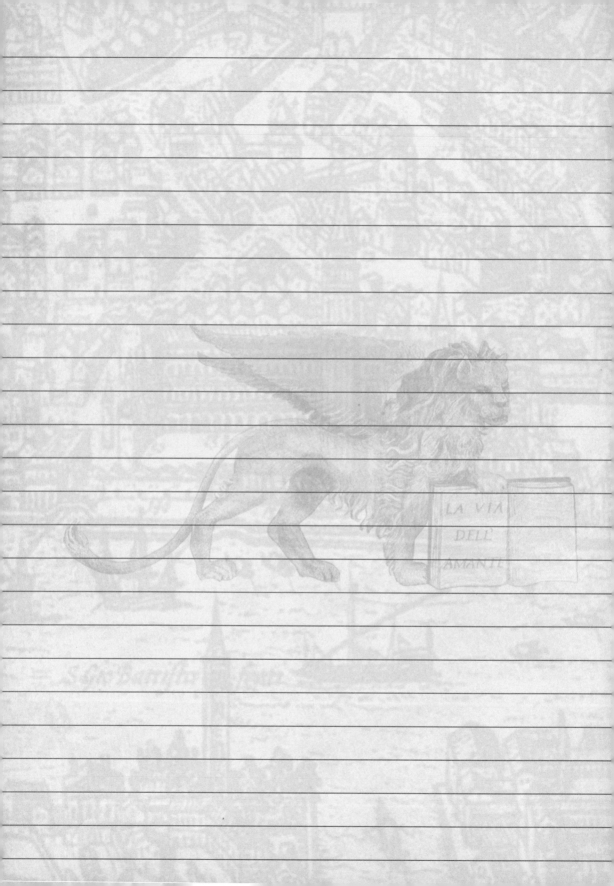

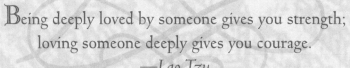

Being deeply loved by someone gives you strength;
loving someone deeply gives you courage.
—Lao Tzu

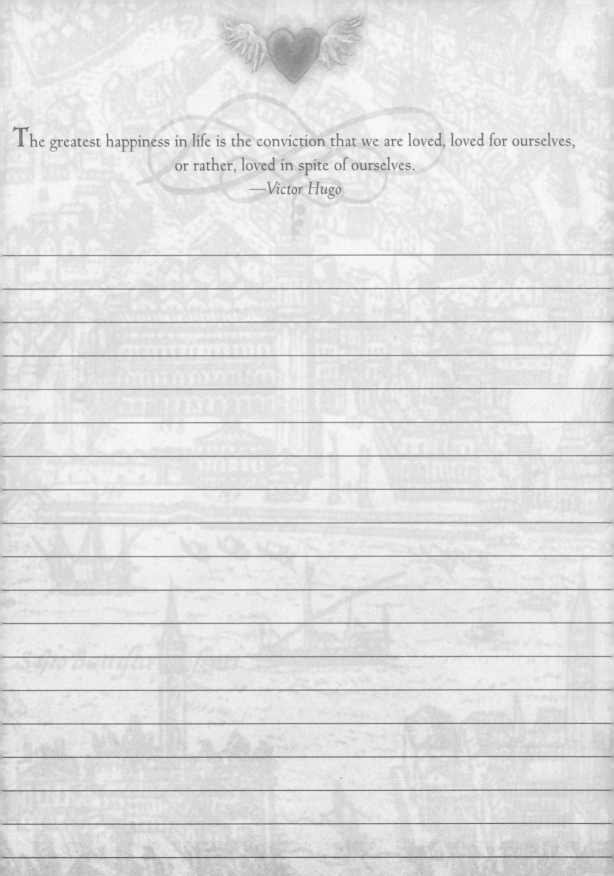

The greatest happiness in life is the conviction that we are loved, loved for ourselves, or rather, loved in spite of ourselves.
—*Victor Hugo*

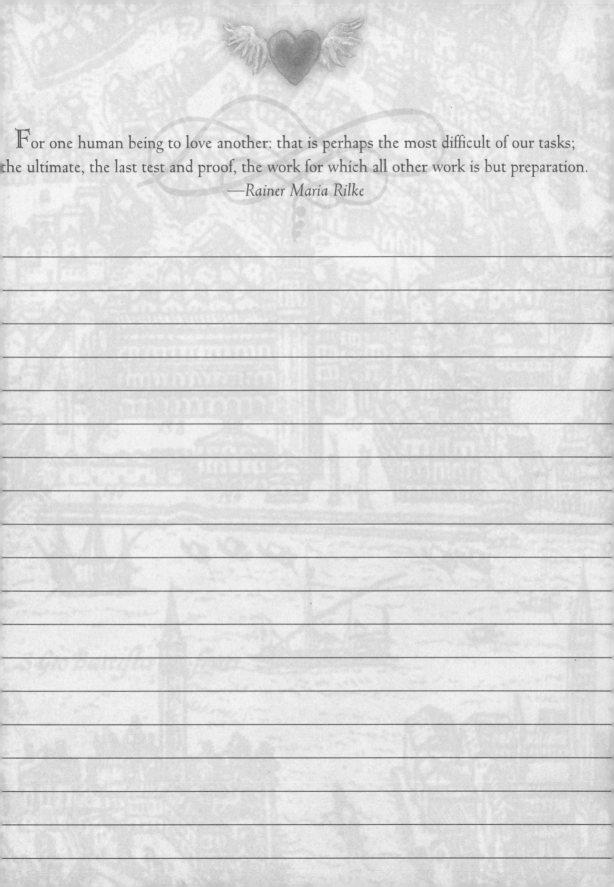

For one human being to love another: that is perhaps the most difficult of our tasks; the ultimate, the last test and proof, the work for which all other work is but preparation.
—*Rainer Maria Rilke*

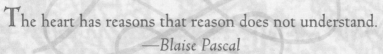

The heart has reasons that reason does not understand.
—*Blaise Pascal*

_____

_____

_____

_____

_____

_____

_____

_____

_____

_____

_____

_____

_____

_____

_____

_____

_____

_____

_____

What greater thing is there for two human souls than to feel that they are joined together to strengthen each other in all labour, to minister to each other in all sorrow, to share with each other in all gladness, to be one with each other in the silent unspoken memories?

—*George Elliot*

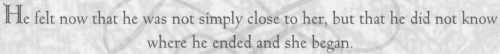

He felt now that he was not simply close to her, but that he did not know
where he ended and she began.
—*Leo Tolstoy*

_____

_____

_____

_____

_____

_____

_____

_____

_____

_____

_____

_____

_____

_____

_____

_____

_____

_____

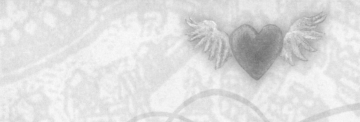

Love is a canvas furnished by Nature and embroidered by imagination.
—*Voltaire*

Love is the joy of the good, the wonder of the wise, the amazement of the gods.
—*Plato*

_____

_____

_____

_____

_____

_____

_____

_____

_____

_____

_____

_____

_____

_____

_____

_____

_____

_____

_____

_____

_____

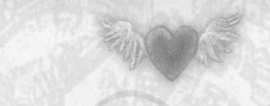

At the touch of love, everyone becomes a poet.
—*Plato*

_____

_____

_____

_____

_____

_____

_____

_____

_____

_____

_____

_____

_____

_____

_____

_____

_____

_____

_____

_____

_____

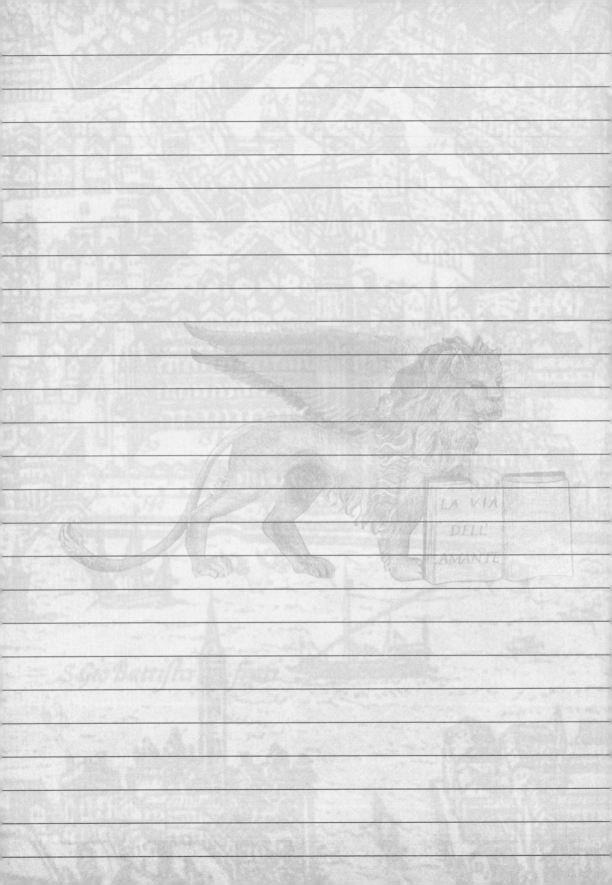

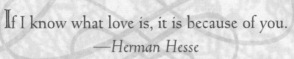

If I know what love is, it is because of you.
—*Herman Hesse*

Love cannot endure indifference. It needs to be wanted. Like a lamp, it needs to be fed out of the oil of another's heart, or its flame burns low.
—*Henry Ward Beecher*

_____
_____
_____
_____
_____
_____
_____
_____
_____
_____
_____
_____
_____
_____
_____
_____
_____
_____
_____
_____

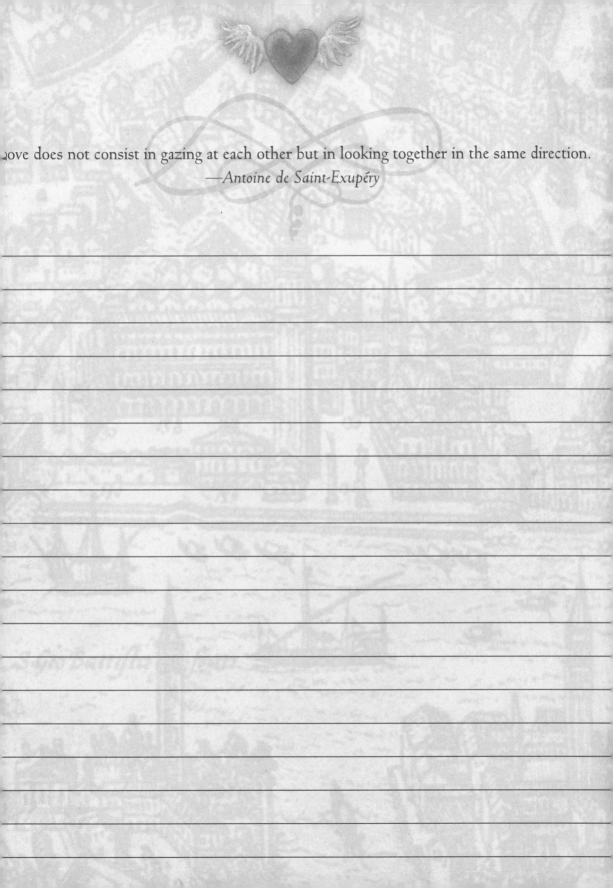

Love does not consist in gazing at each other but in looking together in the same direction.
—*Antoine de Saint-Exupéry*

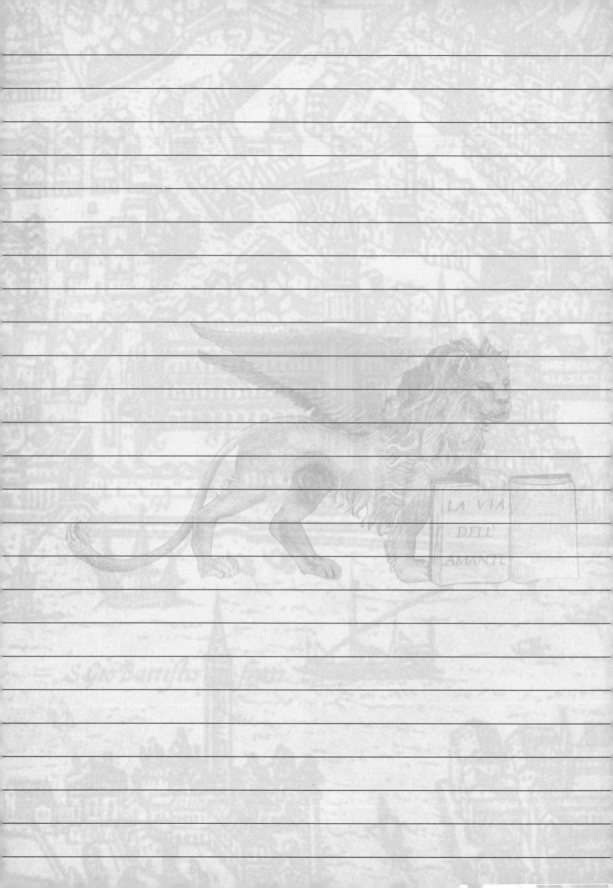

There is no instinct like that of the heart.
—Lord Byron

_____
_____
_____
_____
_____
_____
_____
_____
_____
_____
_____
_____
_____
_____
_____
_____
_____
_____
_____
_____
_____

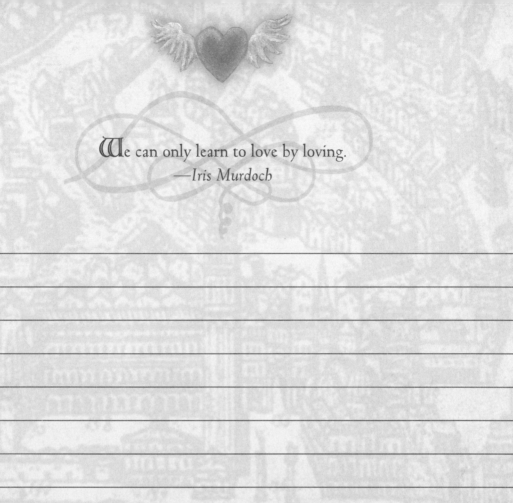

We can only learn to love by loving.
—*Iris Murdoch*

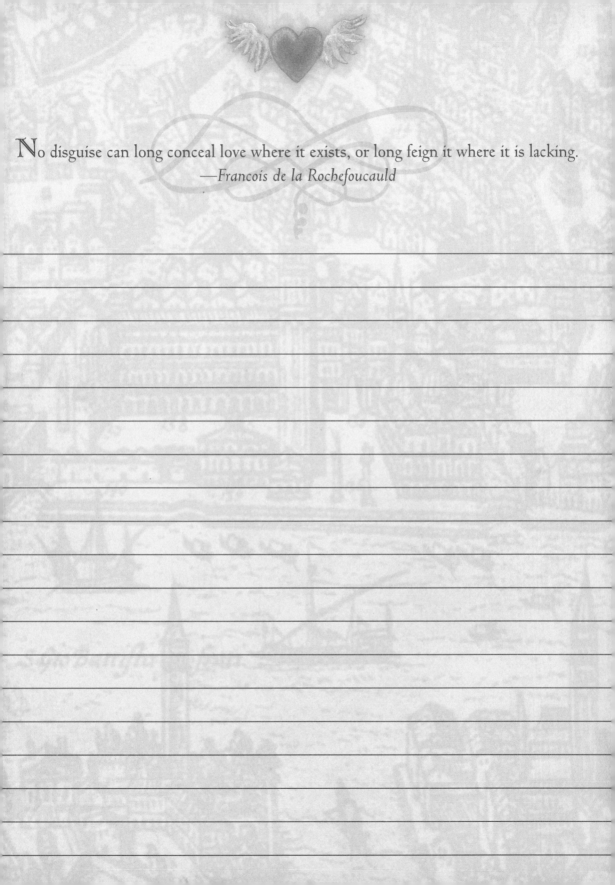

No disguise can long conceal love where it exists, or long feign it where it is lacking.
—Francois de la Rochefoucauld

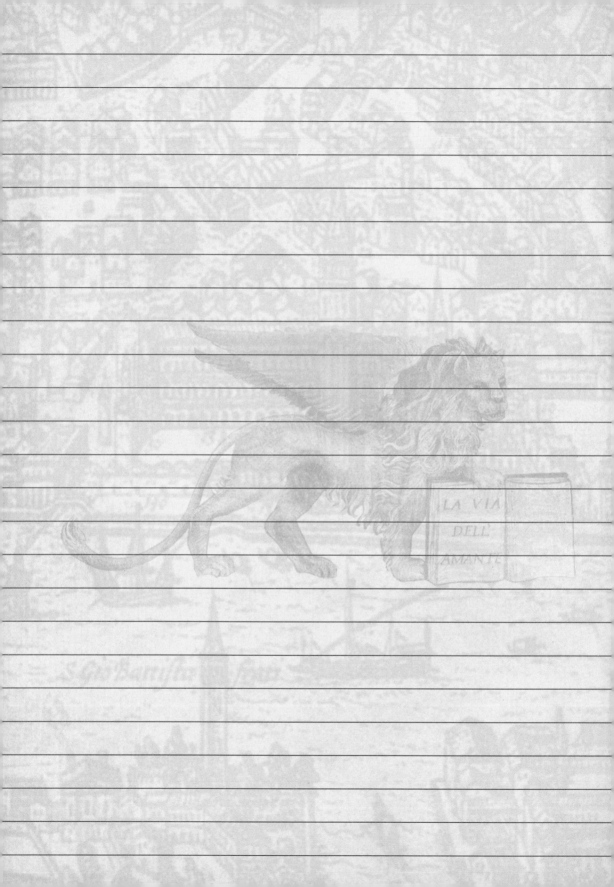

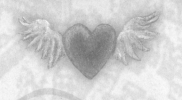

Love is like the moon: if it does not grow bigger, it will grow smaller.
—*Chinese Proverb*

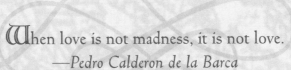

When love is not madness, it is not love.
—*Pedro Calderon de la Barca*

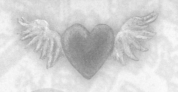

Whatever our souls are made of, his and mine are the same.
—Emily Brontë

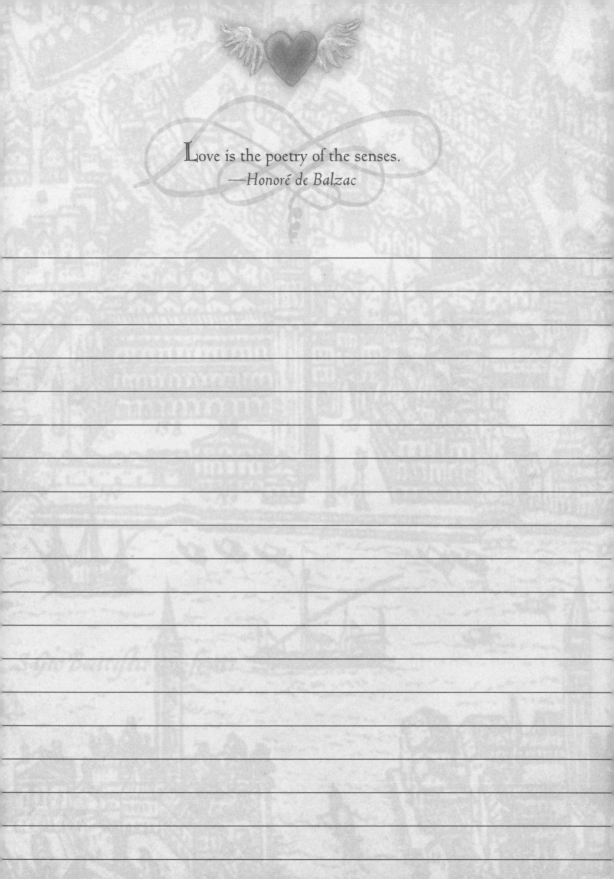

Love is the poetry of the senses.
—Honoré de Balzac

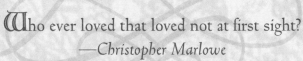

Who ever loved that loved not at first sight?
—*Christopher Marlowe*

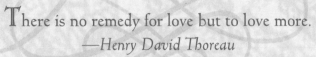

There is no remedy for love but to love more.
—Henry David Thoreau

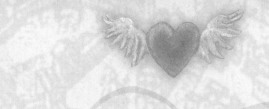

Love looks not with the eyes, but with the mind
And therefore is winged Cupid painted blind.
—*William Shakespeare*

_____

_____

_____

_____

_____

_____

_____

_____

_____

_____

_____

_____

_____

_____

_____

_____

_____

_____

_____

_____

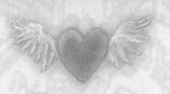

Love has features which pierce all hearts, he wears a bandage which conceals the faults of those beloved. He has wings, he comes quickly and flies away the same.
—*Voltaire*

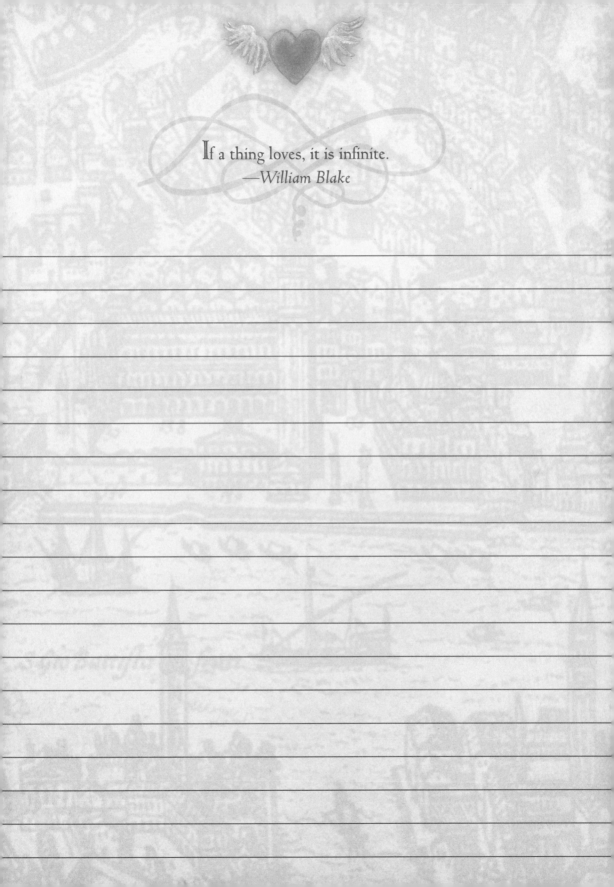

If a thing loves, it is infinite.
—*William Blake*

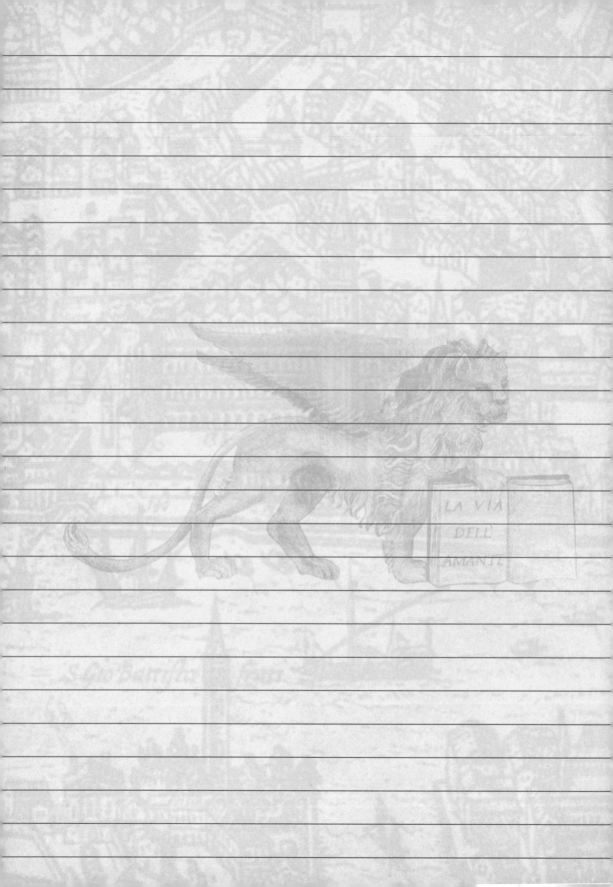

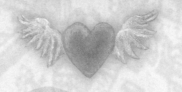

Accept the things to which fate binds you, and love the people with whom fate brings you together, but do so with all your heart.
—*Marcus Aurelius*

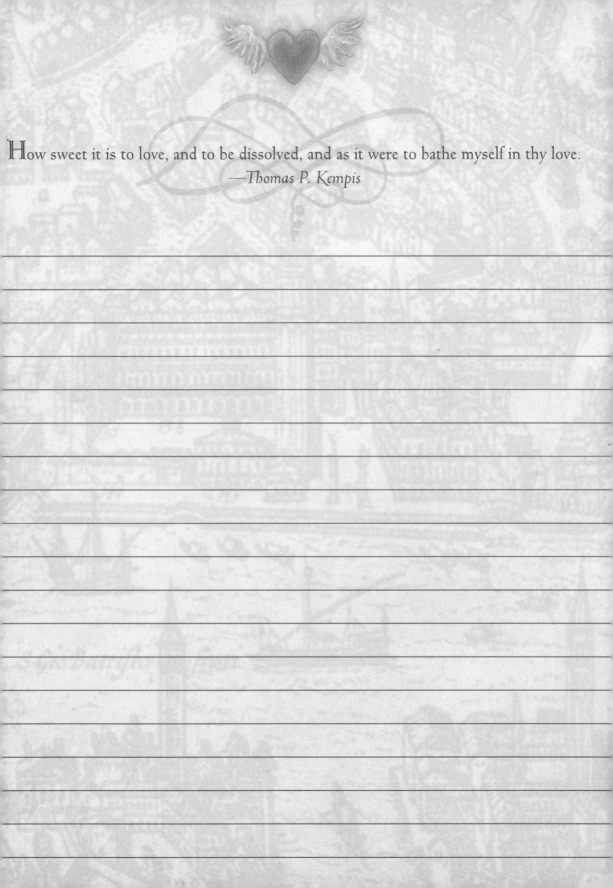

How sweet it is to love, and to be dissolved, and as it were to bathe myself in thy love.
—*Thomas P. Kempis*

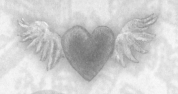

Love means the body, the soul, the life, the entire being. We feel love as we feel the warmth of our blood, we breathe love as we breathe air, we hold it in ourselves as we hold our thoughts. Nothing more exists for us.
—*Guy de Maupassant*

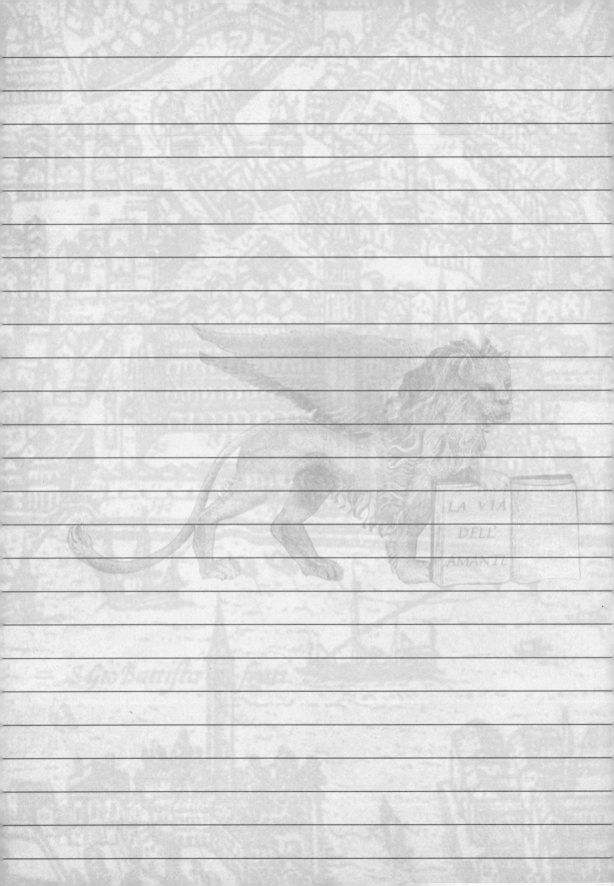

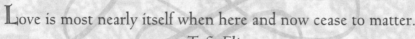

Love is most nearly itself when here and now cease to matter.
—T. S. Eliot

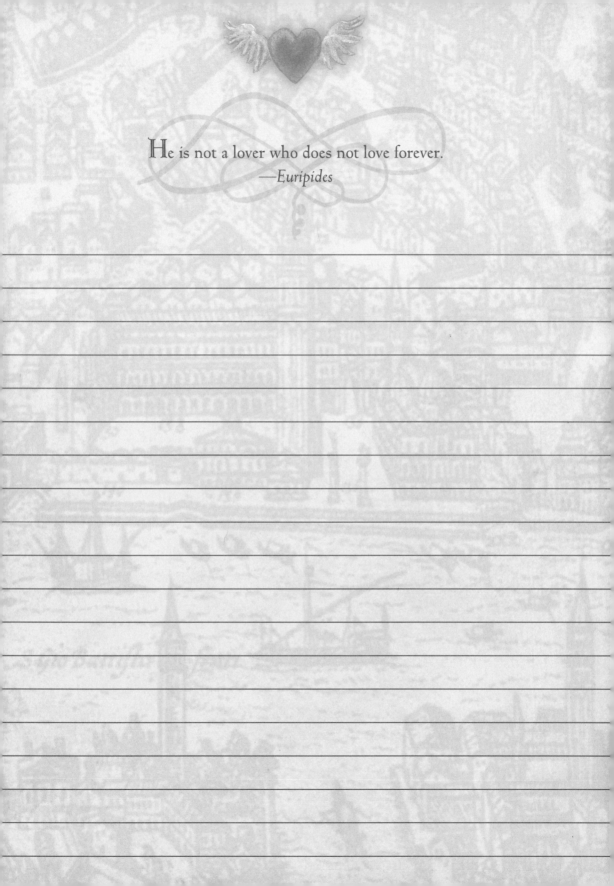

He is not a lover who does not love forever.
—Euripides

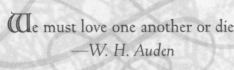

We must love one another or die.
—W. H. Auden

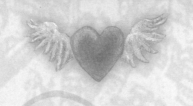

The motto of chivalry is also the motto of wisdom; to serve all, but love only one.
—*Honoré de Balzac*

_____

_____

_____

_____

_____

_____

_____

_____

_____

_____

_____

_____

_____

_____

_____

_____

_____

_____

_____

_____

_____

_____

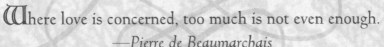

Where love is concerned, too much is not even enough.
—*Pierre de Beaumarchais*

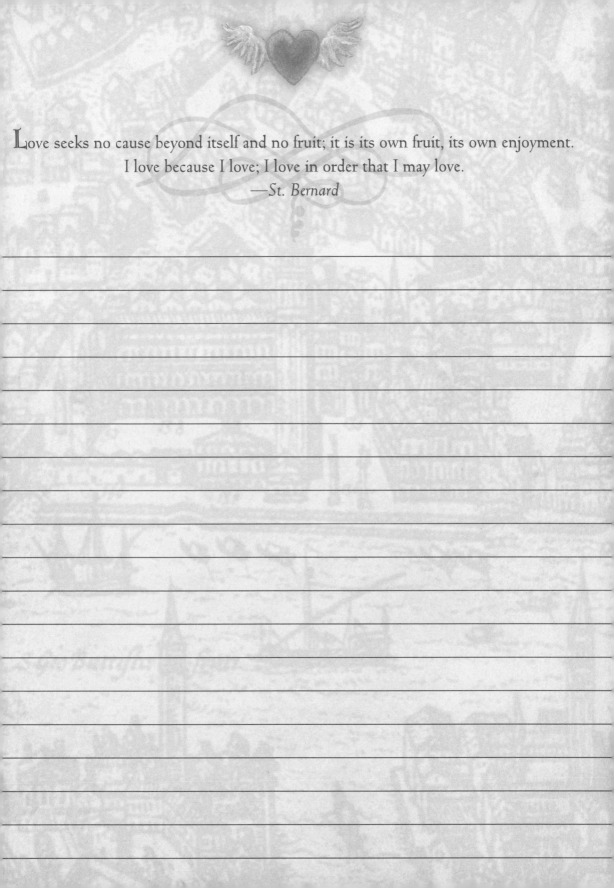

Love seeks no cause beyond itself and no fruit; it is its own fruit, its own enjoyment. I love because I love; I love in order that I may love.

—*St. Bernard*

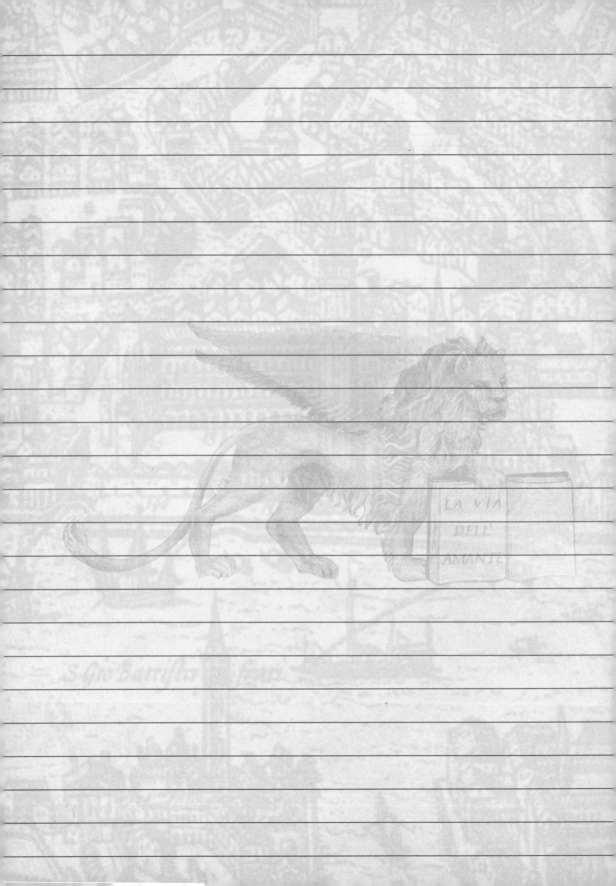

Love thou the rose, yet leave it on its stem.
—*Edward G. Bulwer-Lytton*

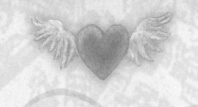

Love is not altogether a delirium, yet it has many points in common therewith.
—*Thomas Carlyle*

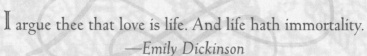

I argue thee that love is life. And life hath immortality.
—*Emily Dickinson*

_____

_____

_____

_____

_____

_____

_____

_____

_____

_____

_____

_____

_____

_____

_____

_____

_____

_____

_____

_____

_____

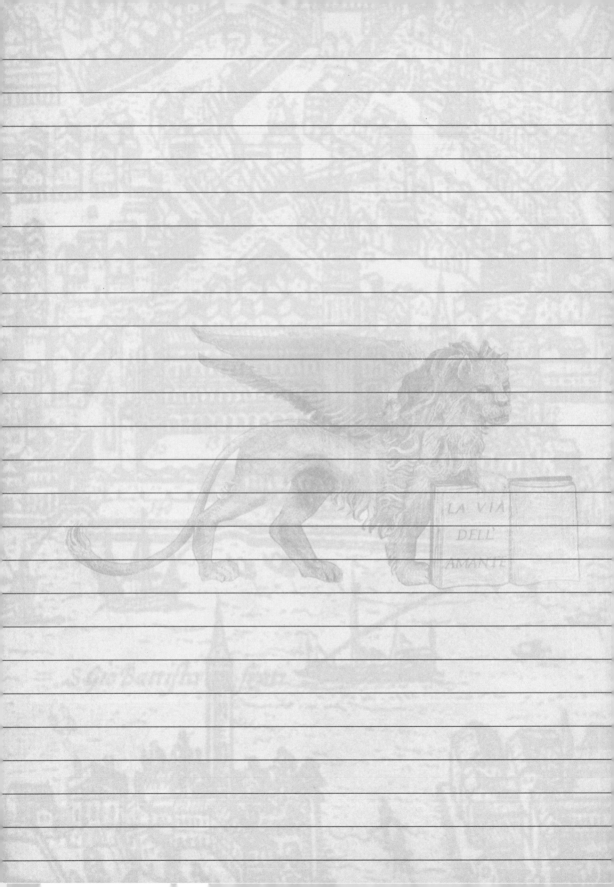

Love, all alike, no season knows, nor clime, nor hours, days, months,
which are the rags of time.
—*John Donne*

That is the true season of love; when we believe that we alone can love, that no one could ever have loved as much before, and that no one will ever love in the same way again.
—*Johann Wolfgang von Goethe*

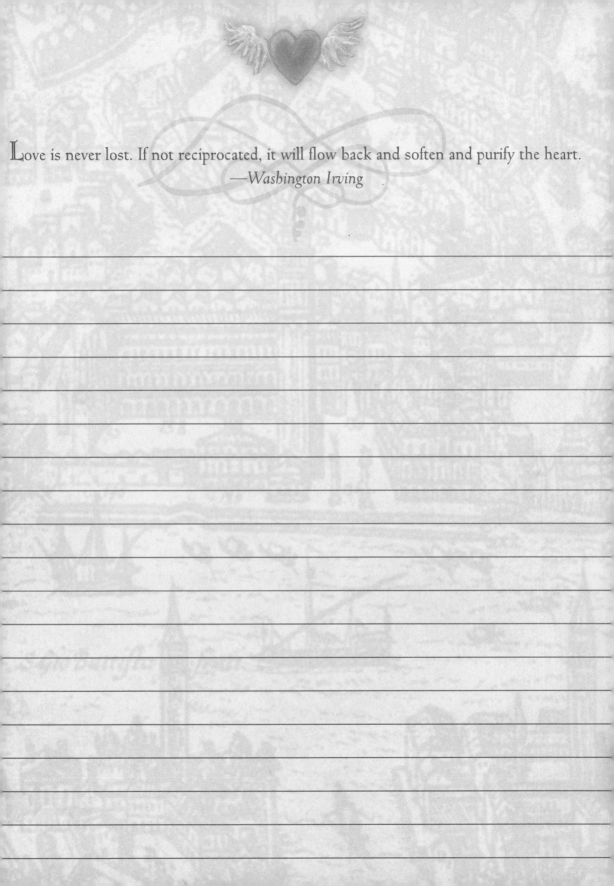

Love is never lost. If not reciprocated, it will flow back and soften and purify the heart.
—*Washington Irving*

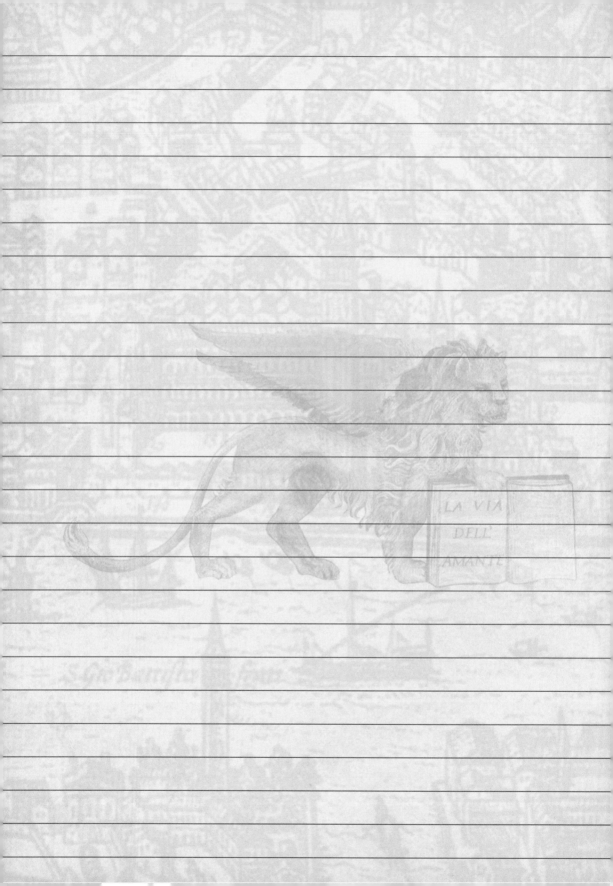

Nothing is more beautiful than the love that has weathered the storms of life. The love of the young for the young, that is the beginning of life. But the love of the old for the old, that is the beginning of things longer.

—Jerome K. Jerome

Neither a lofty degree of intelligence nor imagination nor both together go to the making of genius. Love, love, love, that is the soul of genius.
—*Wolfgang Amadeus Mozart*

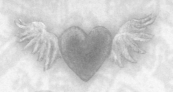

For love . . . has two faces; one white, the other black; two bodies; one smooth, the other hairy. It has two hands, two feet, two tails, two, indeed, of every member and each one is the exact opposite of the other. Yet, so strictly are they joined together.
—*Virginia Woolf*

A very small degree of hope is sufficient to cause the birth of love.
—*Stendhal*

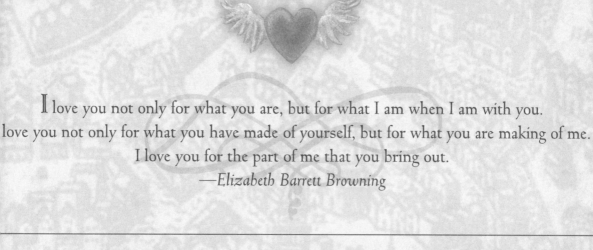

I love you not only for what you are, but for what I am when I am with you.
love you not only for what you have made of yourself, but for what you are making of me.
I love you for the part of me that you bring out.
—*Elizabeth Barrett Browning*

_____

_____

_____

_____

_____

_____

_____

_____

_____

_____

_____

_____

_____

_____

_____

_____

_____

_____

Love is a smoke made with the fume of sighs.
—William Shakespeare

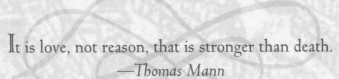

It is love, not reason, that is stronger than death.
—*Thomas Mann*

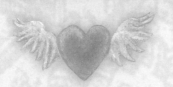

I love you without knowing how, or when, or from where.
I love you straight forwardly without complexities or pride
So close that your hand on my chest is my hand,
so close that your eyes close when I fall asleep.
—*Pablo Neruda*

_____

_____

_____

_____

_____

_____

_____

_____

_____

_____

_____

_____

_____

_____

_____

_____

_____

_____

_____

_____

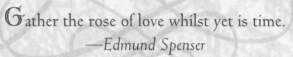

Gather the rose of love whilst yet is time.
—*Edmund Spenser*

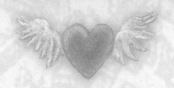

*L*ove many things, for therein lies the true strength, and whosoever loves much performs much, and can accomplish much, and what is done in love is done well.
—*Vincent van Gogh*

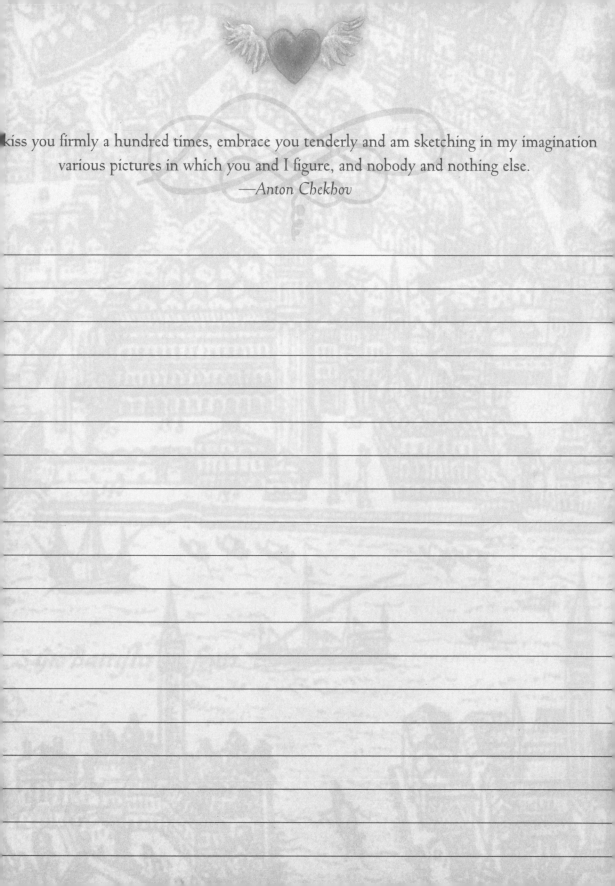

kiss you firmly a hundred times, embrace you tenderly and am sketching in my imagination various pictures in which you and I figure, and nobody and nothing else.
—*Anton Chekhov*

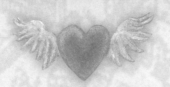

Carry me off into the blue skies of tender loves, roll me dark clouds, trample me with your thunderstorms, break me in your angry rages. But love me, my adored lover.
—*Sarah Bernhardt*

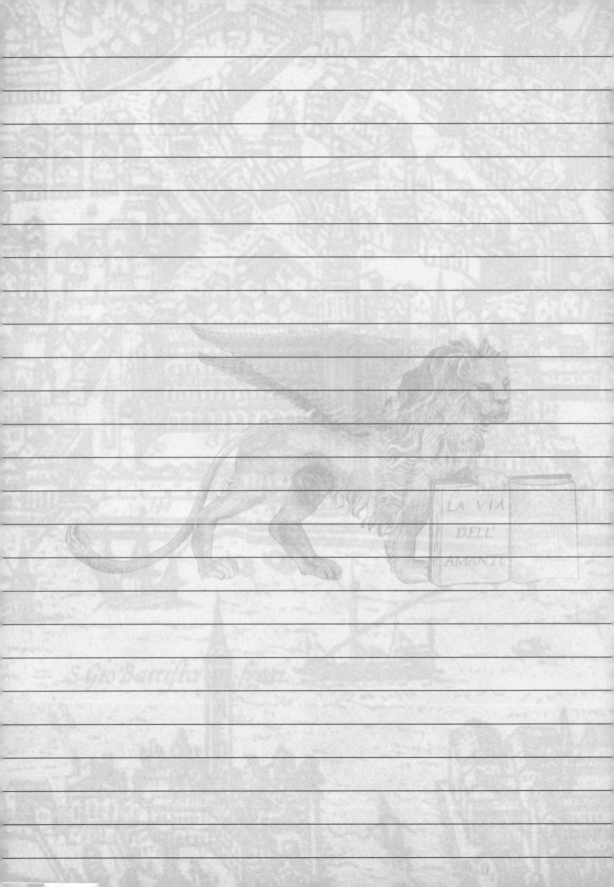

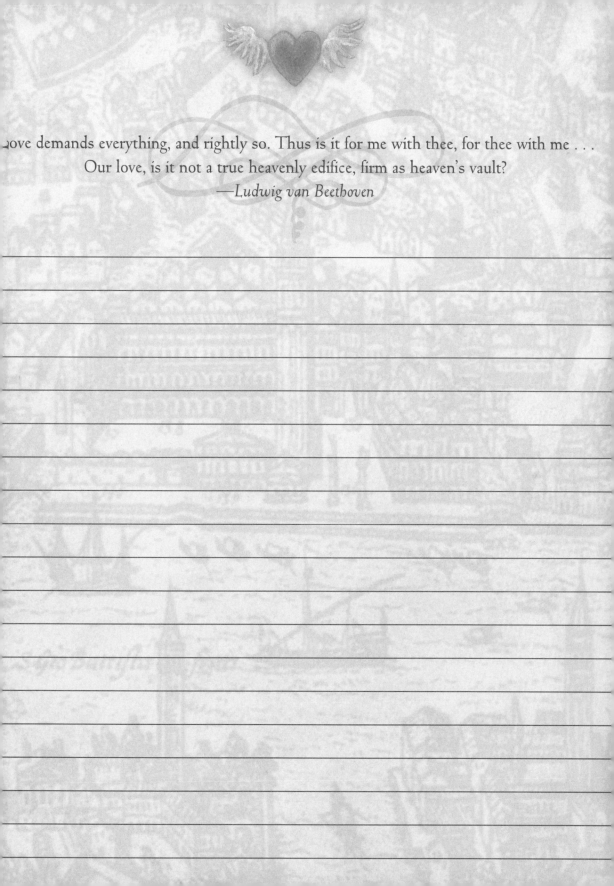

Love demands everything, and rightly so. Thus is it for me with thee, for thee with me . . .
Our love, is it not a true heavenly edifice, firm as heaven's vault?
—*Ludwig van Beethoven*

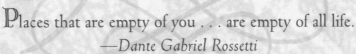

Places that are empty of you . . . are empty of all life.
　　　　　　　—Dante Gabriel Rossetti

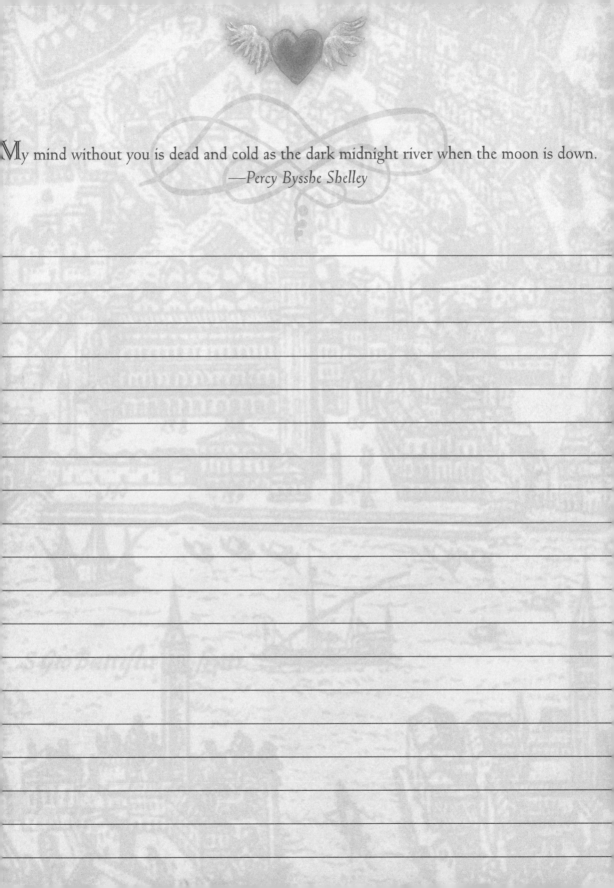

My mind without you is dead and cold as the dark midnight river when the moon is down.
—*Percy Bysshe Shelley*

Only three things are infinite: the sky in its stars, the sea in drops of water, and the heart in its tears.
—*Gustave Flaubert*

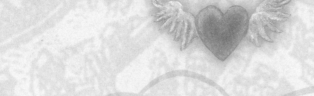

What a happy and holy fashion it is that those who love one another should rest on the same pillow.
—*Nathaniel Hawthorne*

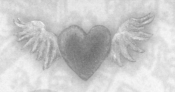

I will come back alive and as deep in love with you as a cormorant dives,
as an anemone grows, as Neptune breathes, as the sea is deep.
—Dylan Thomas

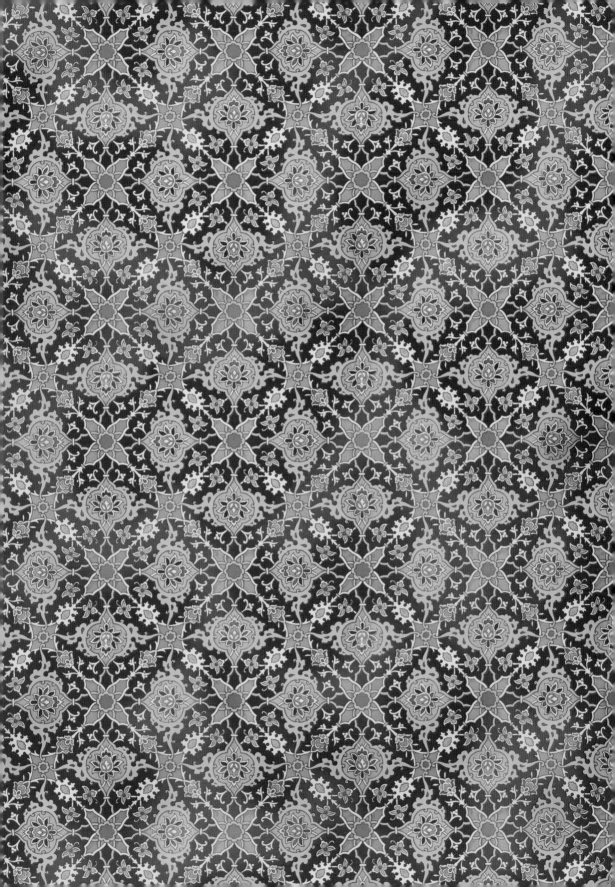

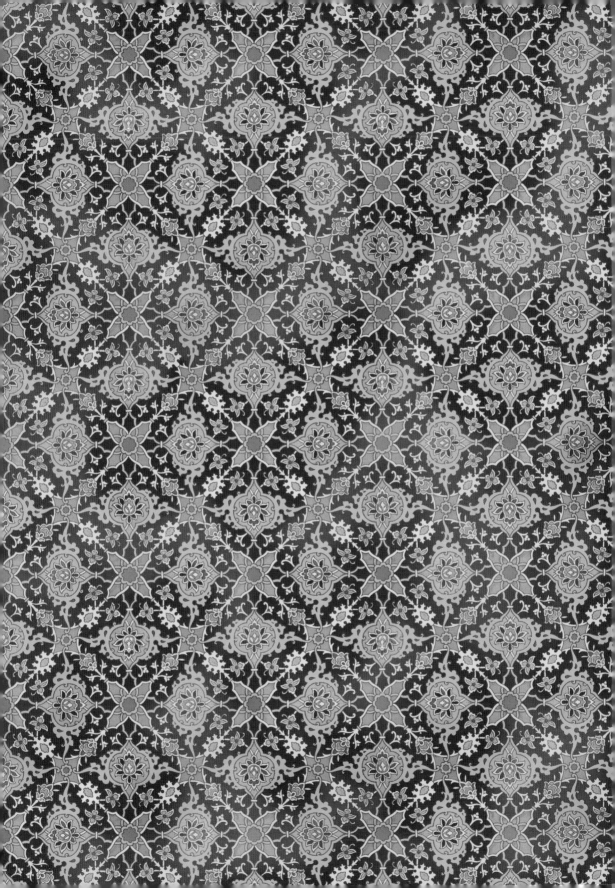